Farting Unicorns

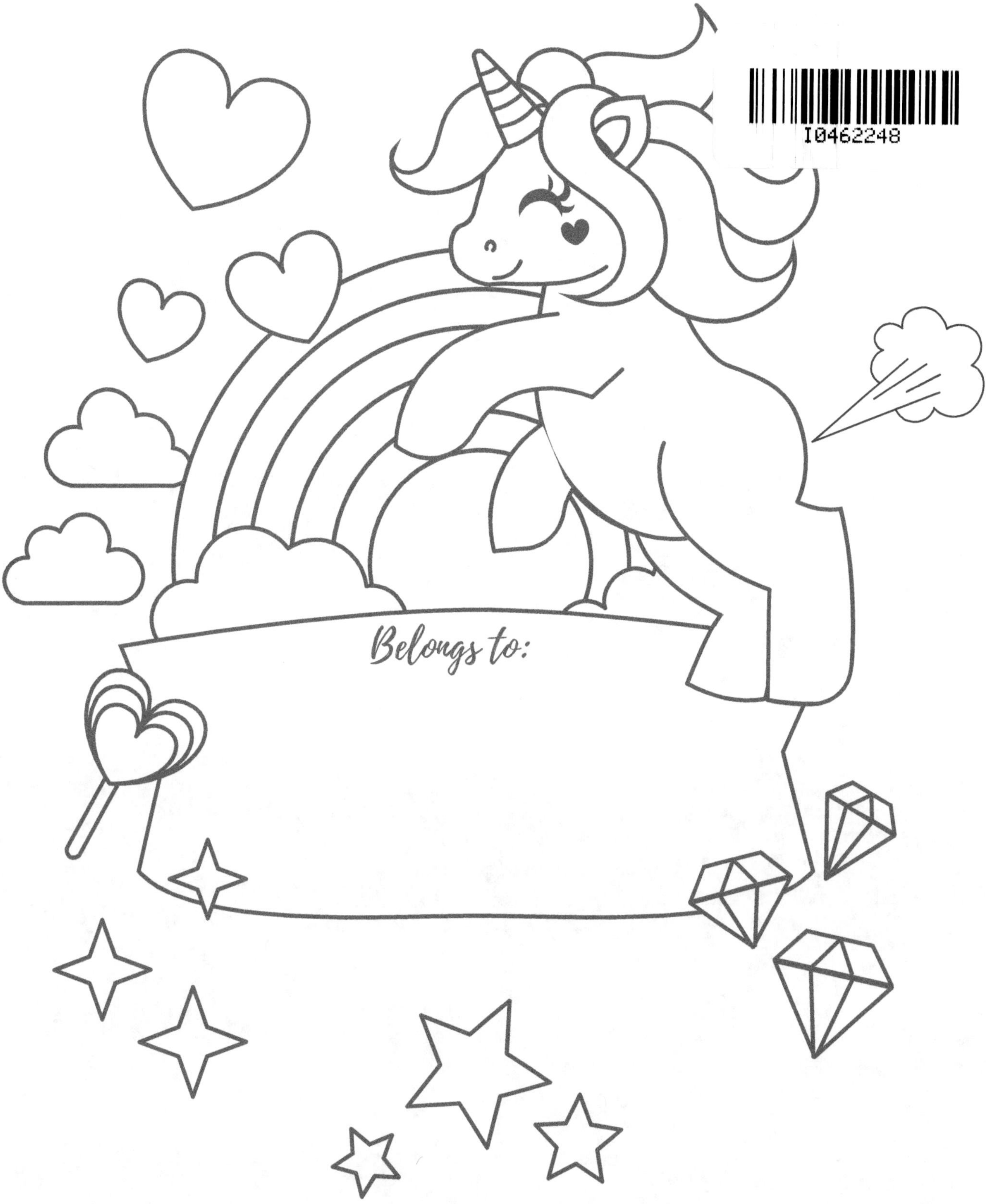

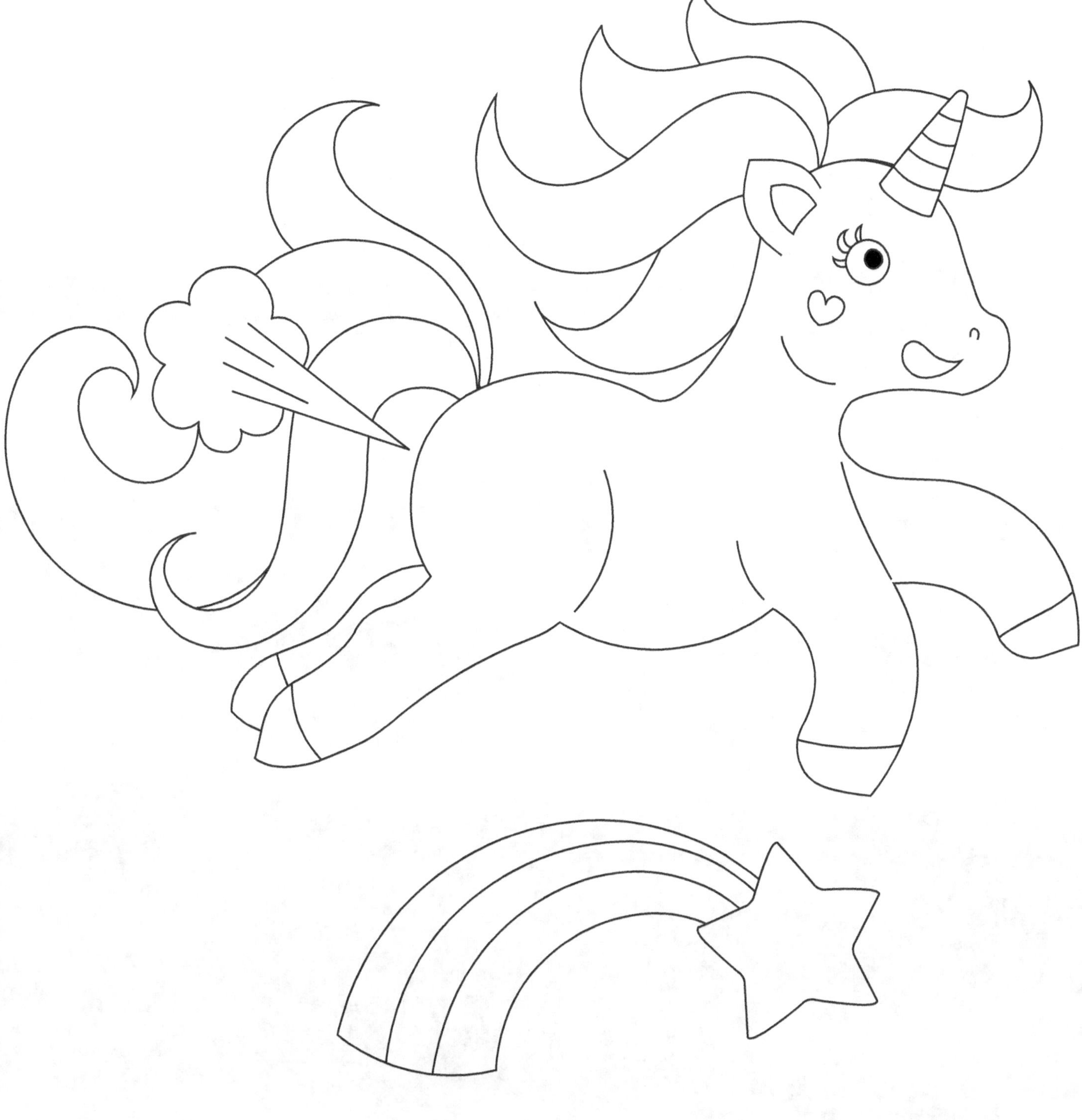

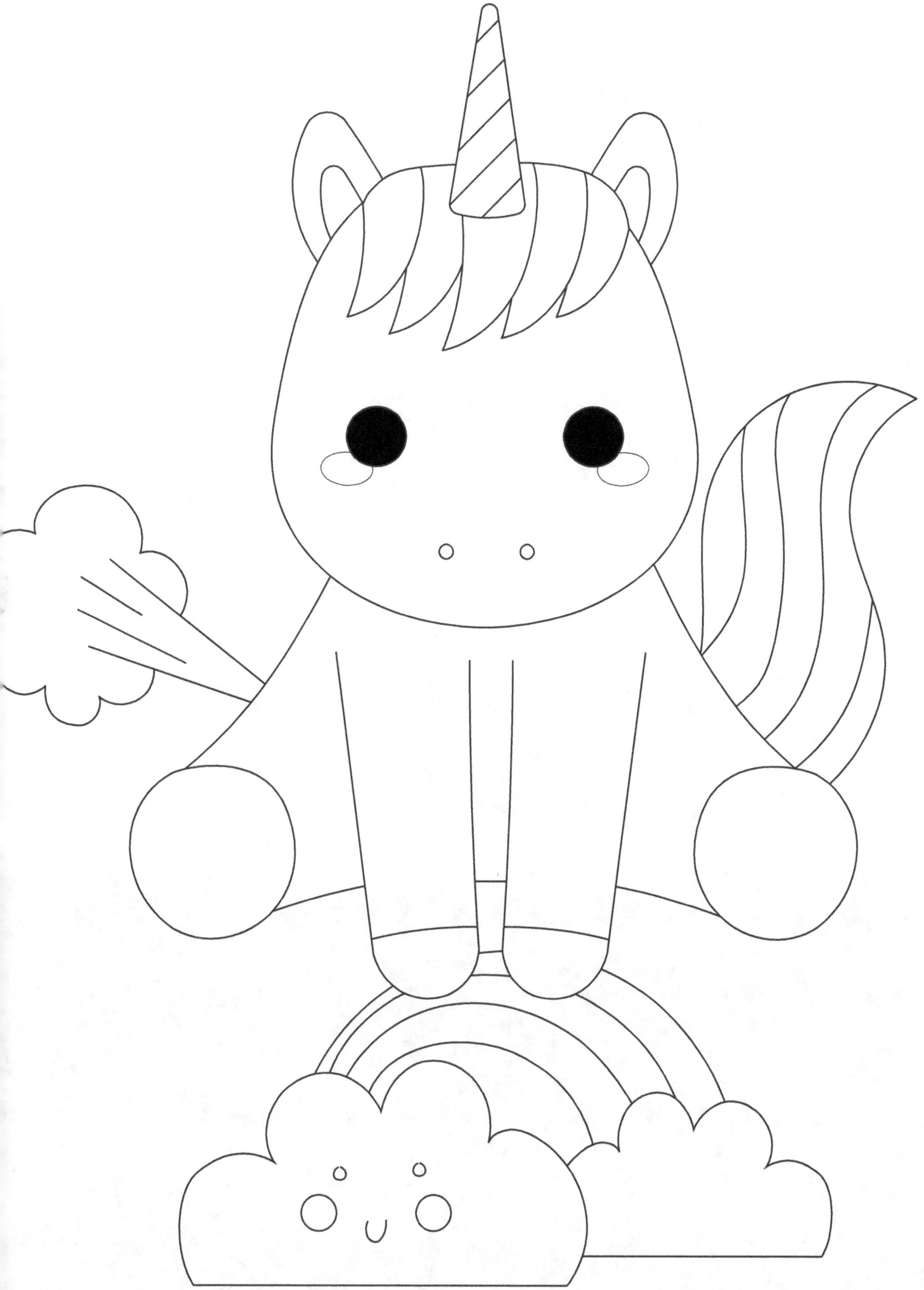

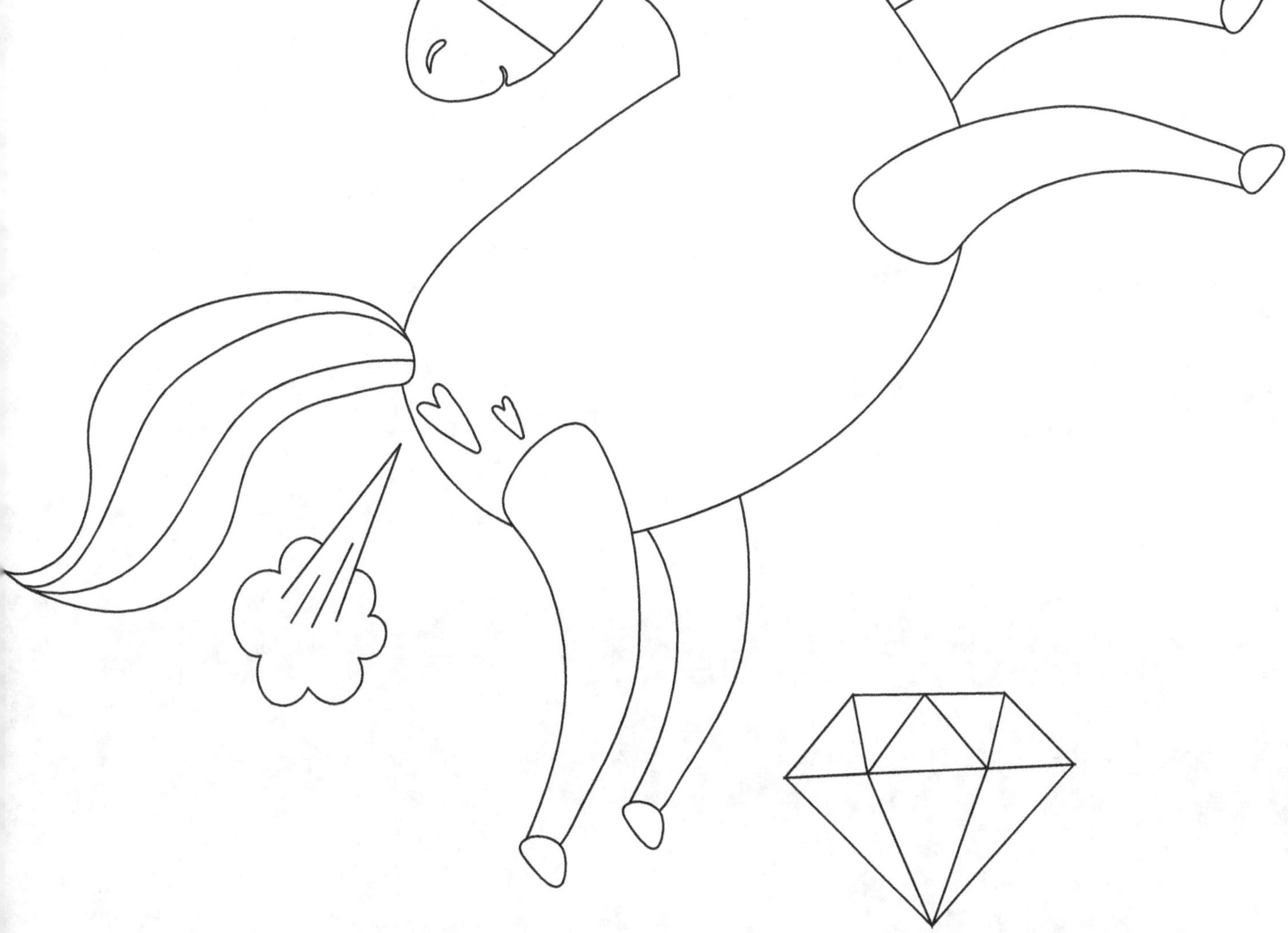

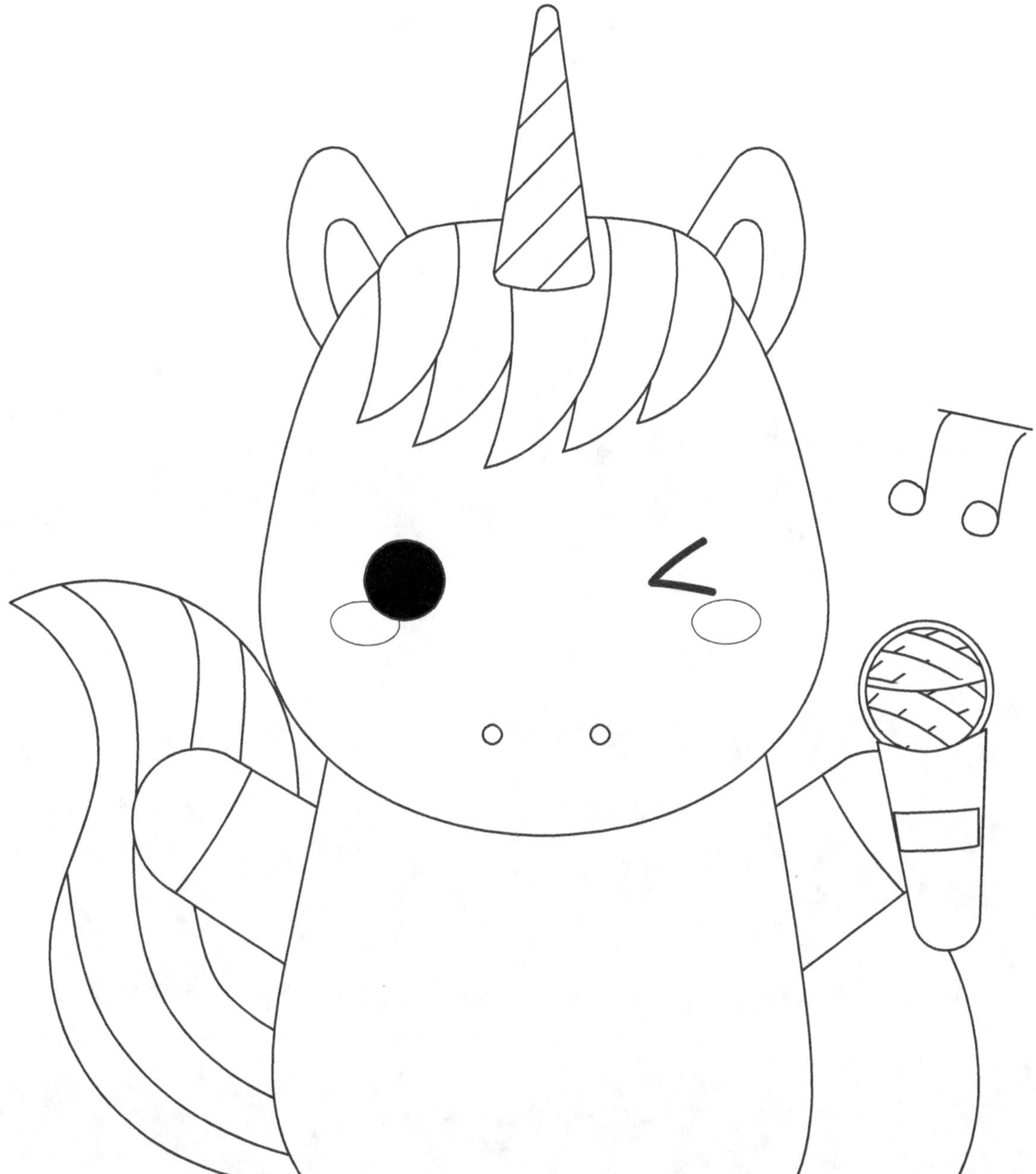

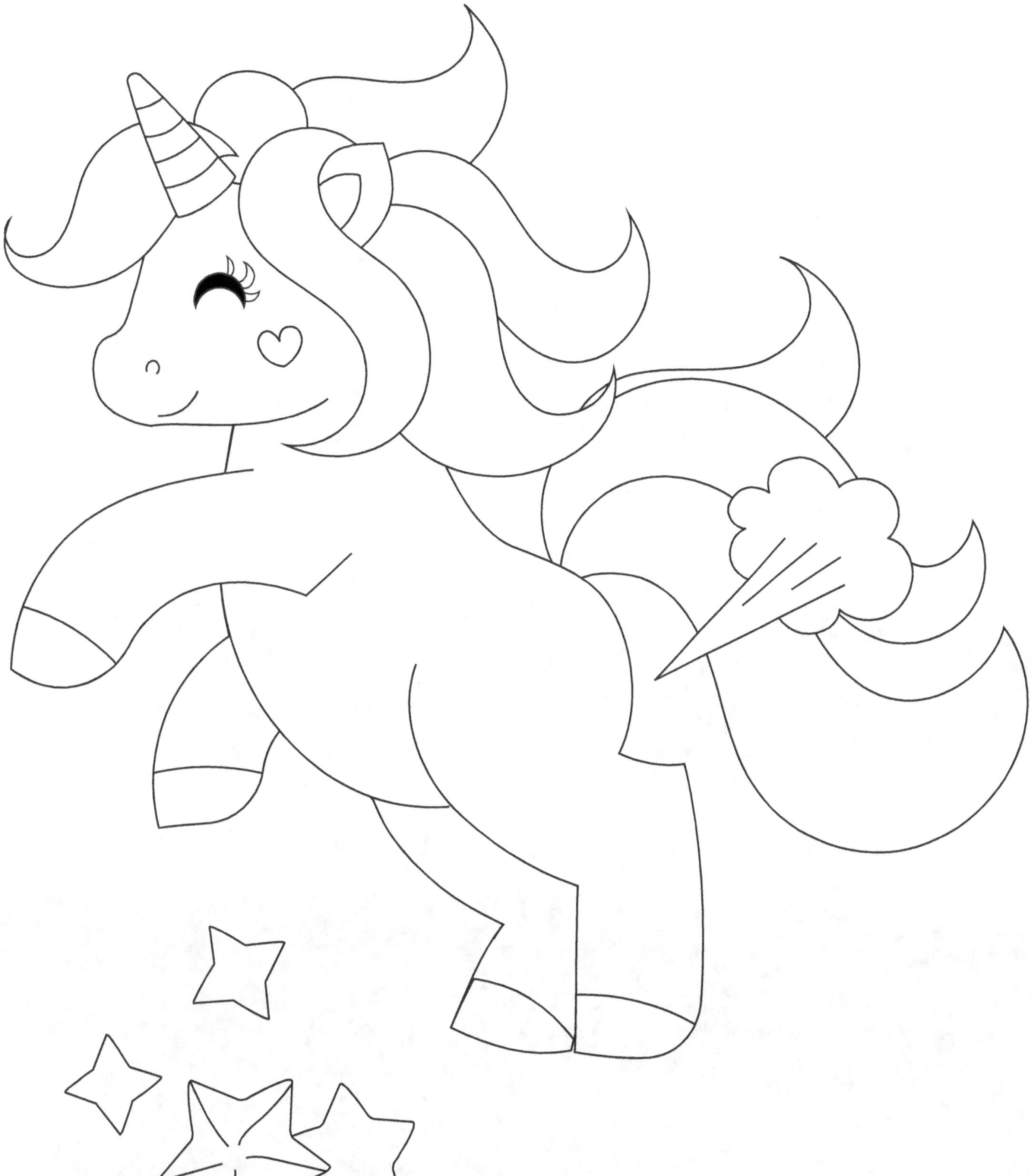

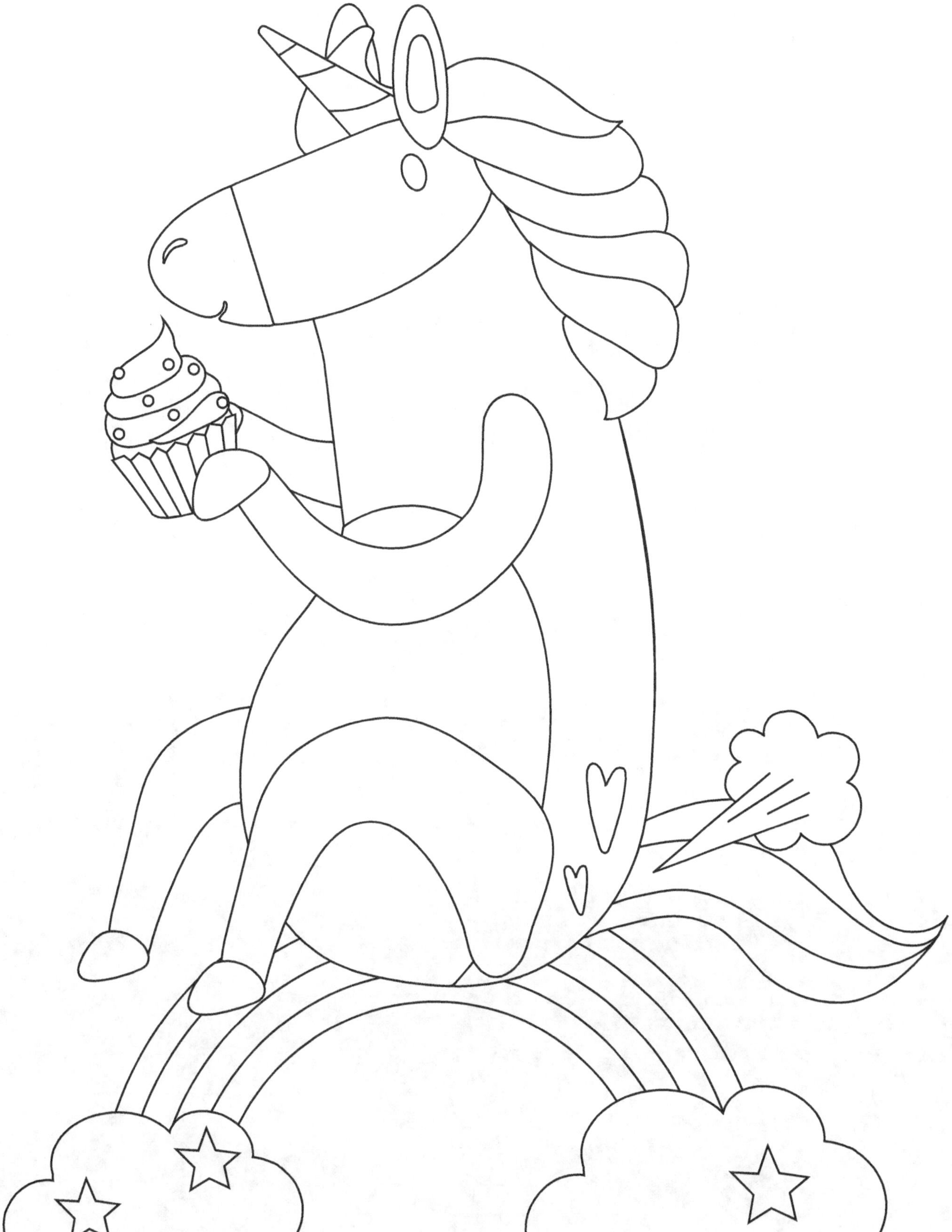

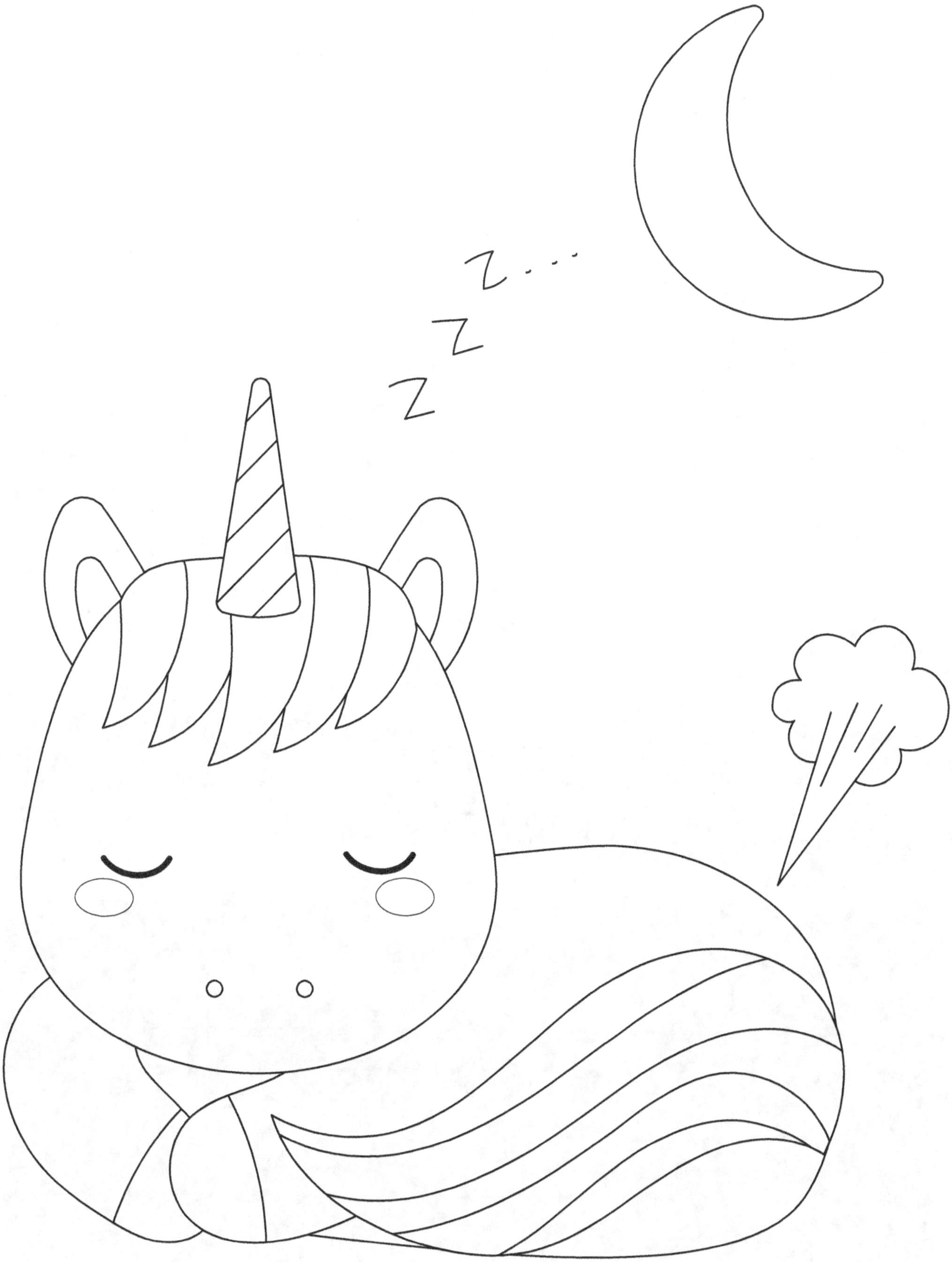
Z Z Z . . .

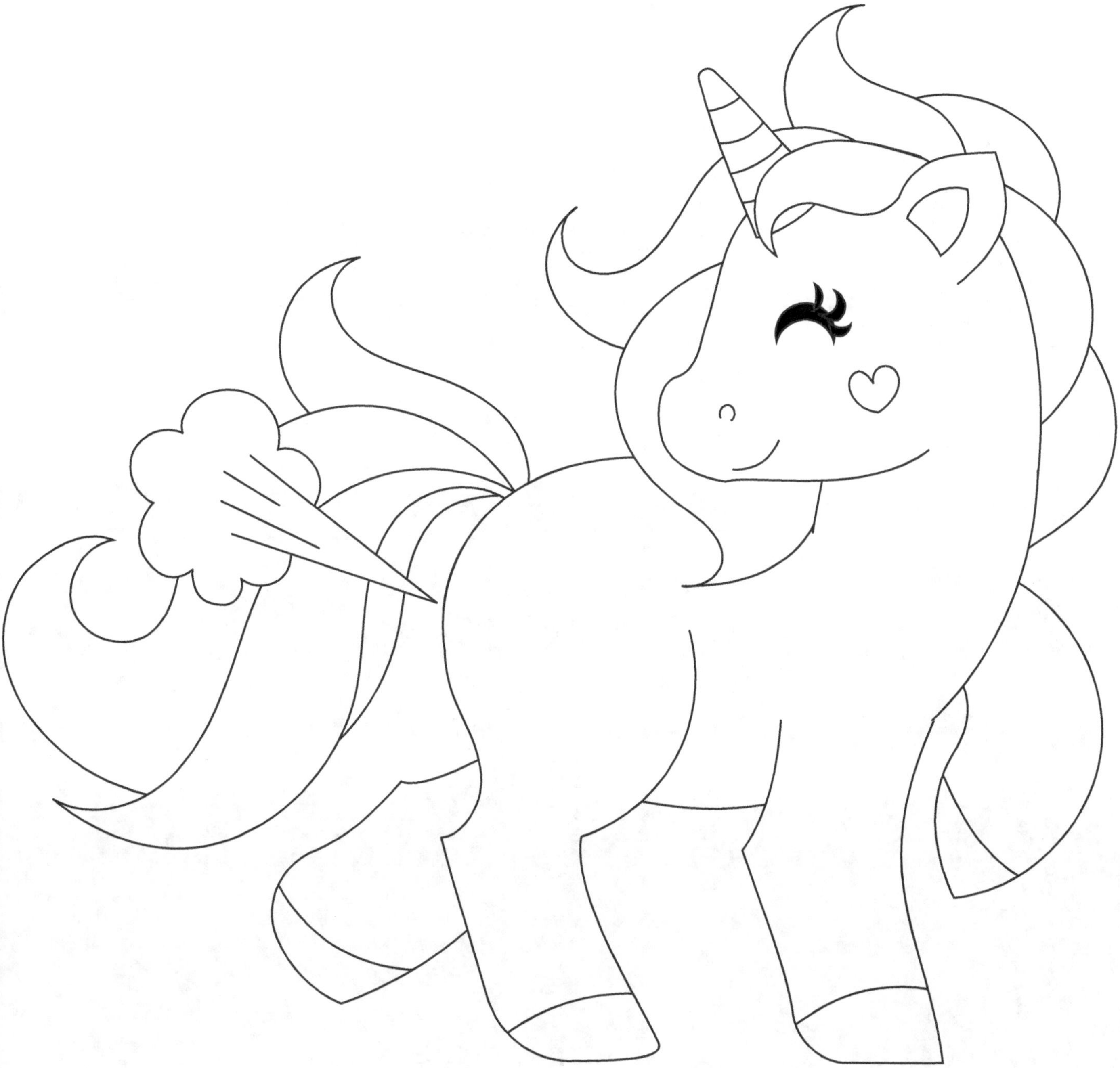

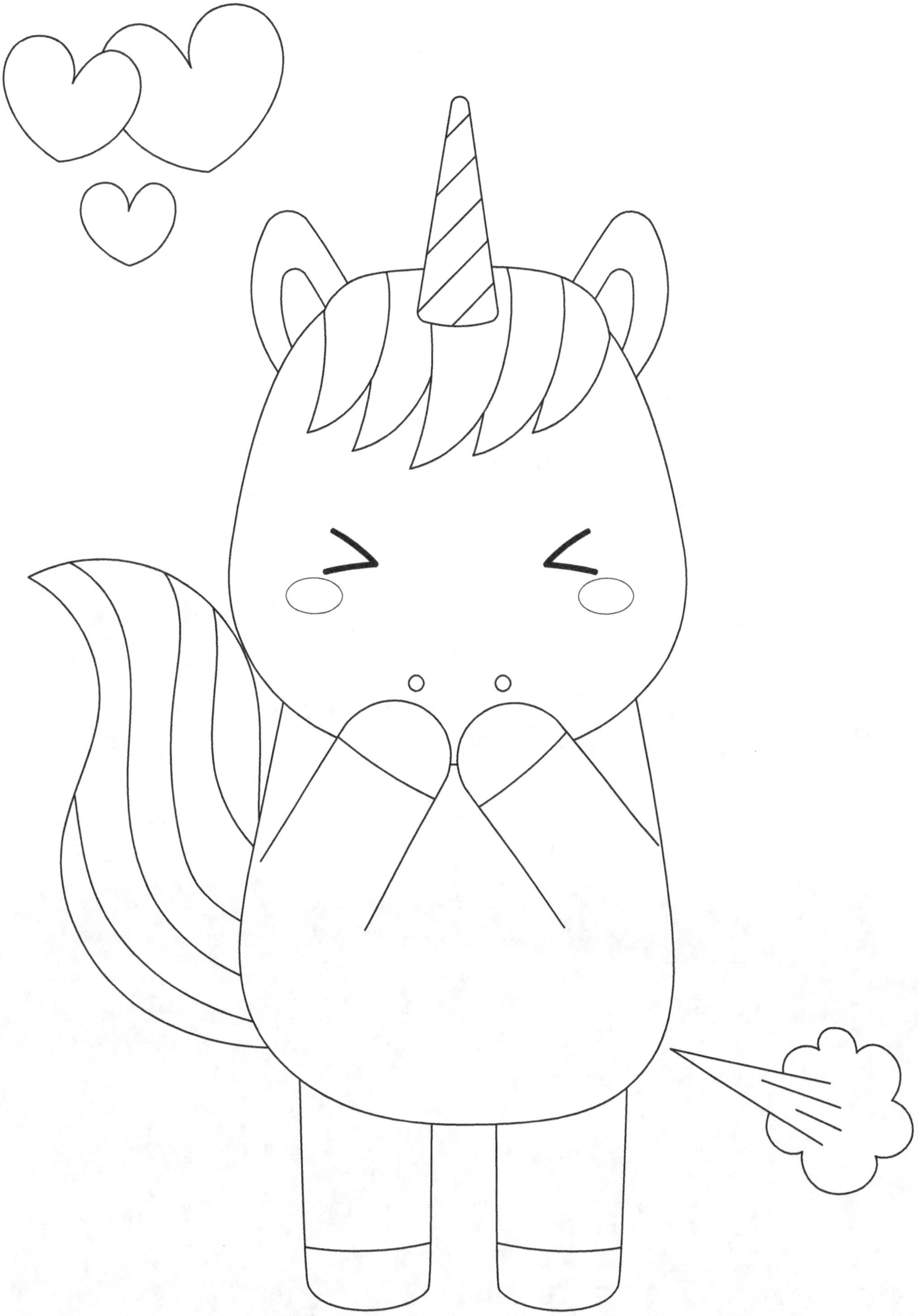

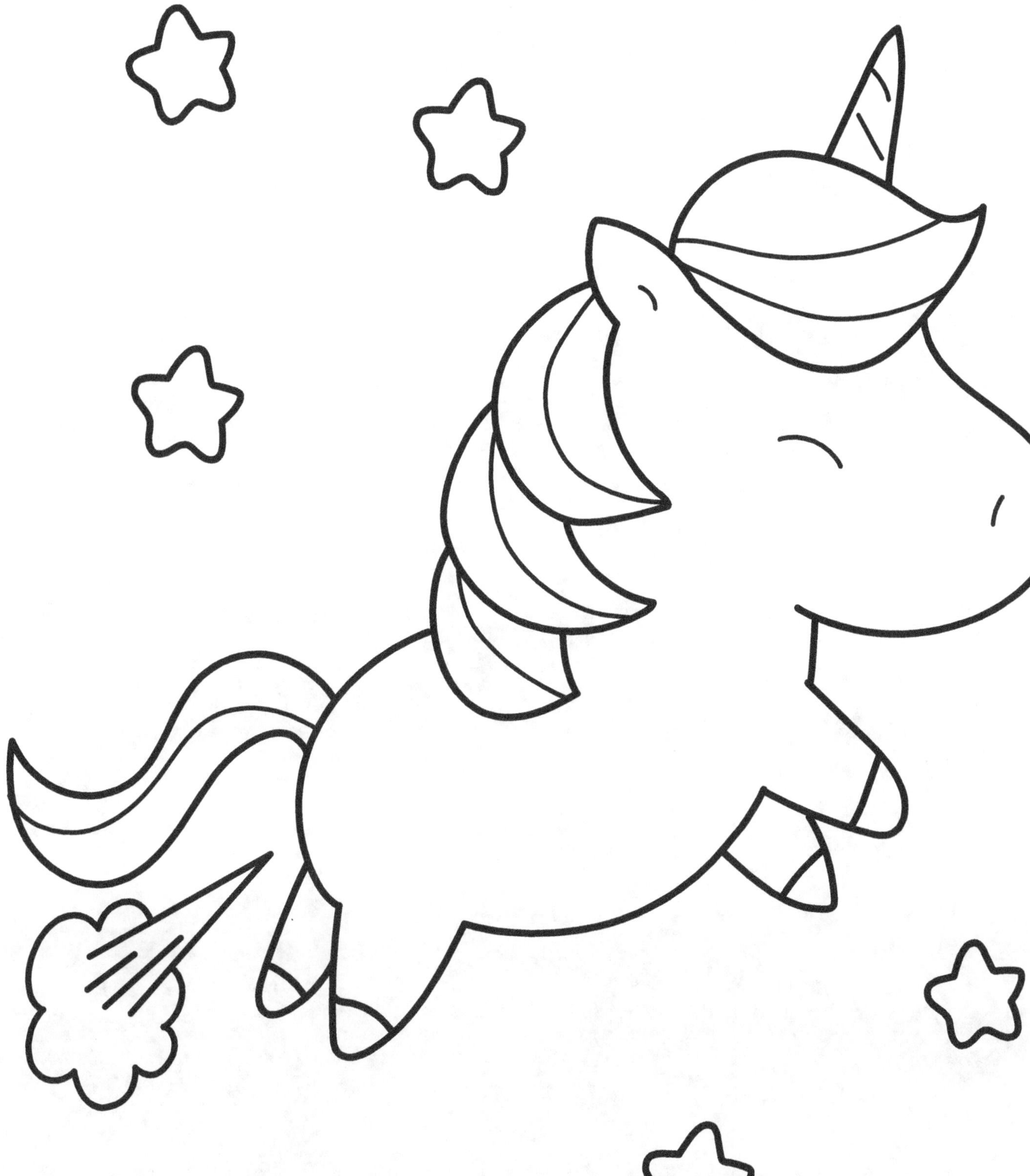

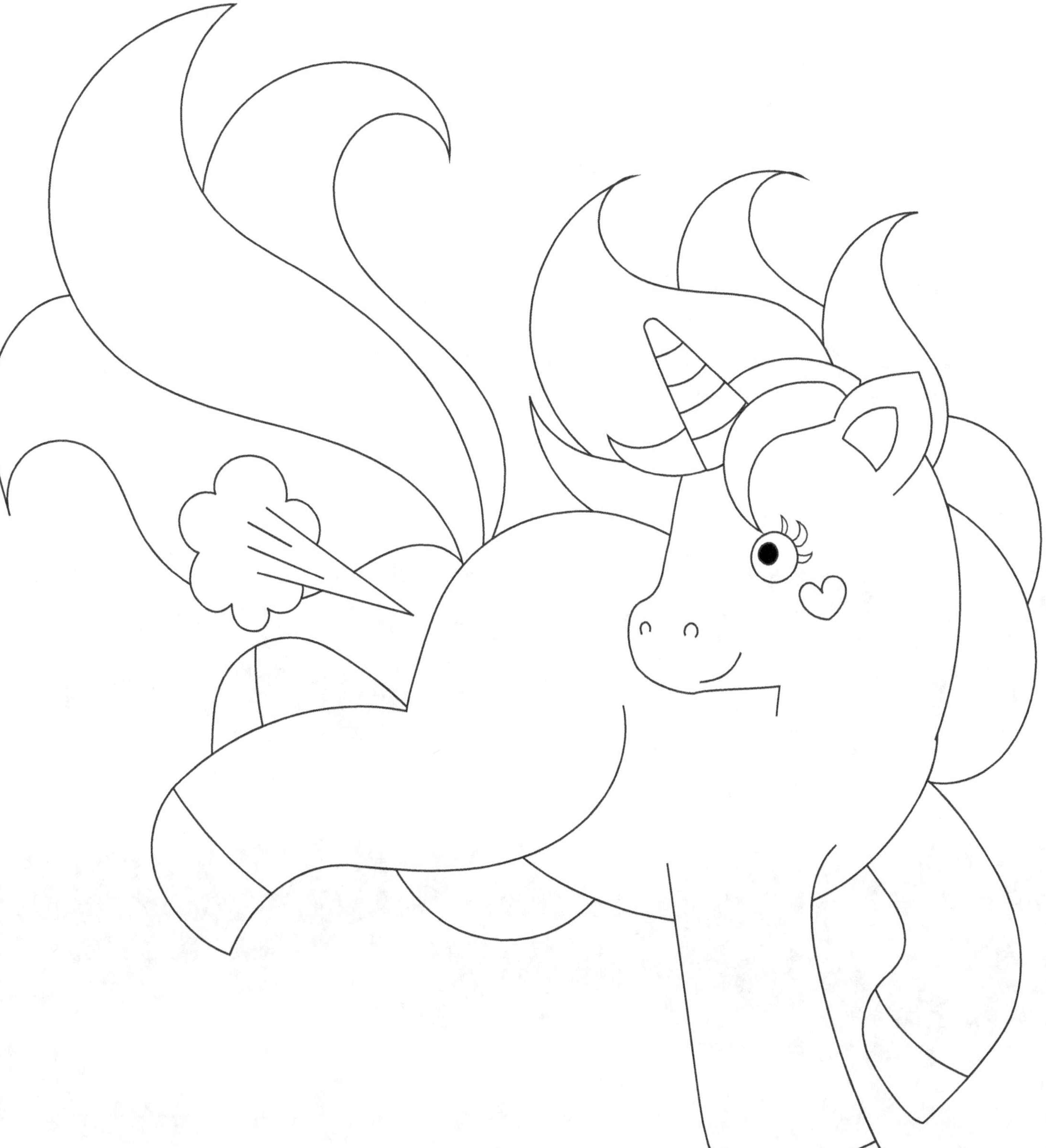

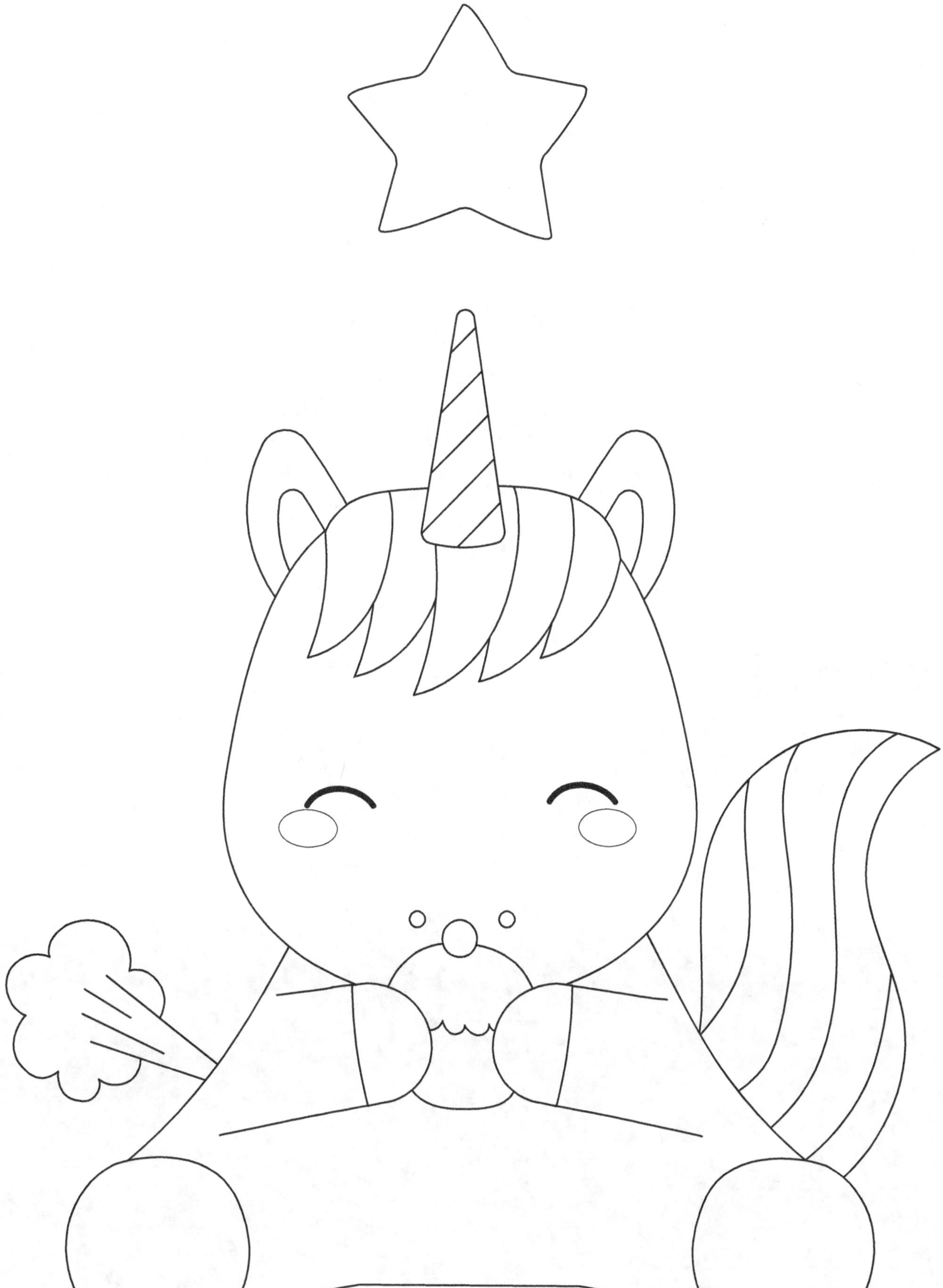

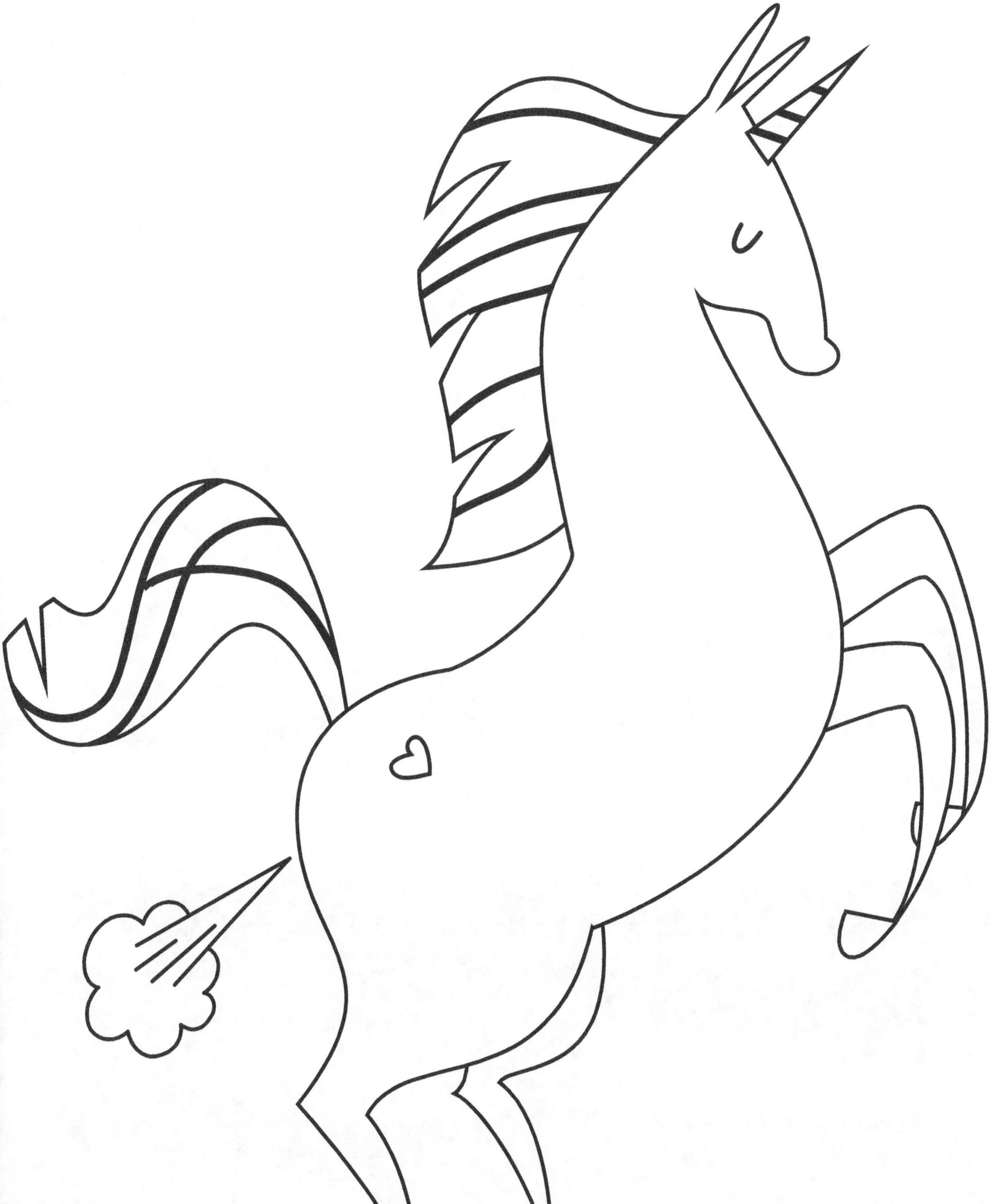

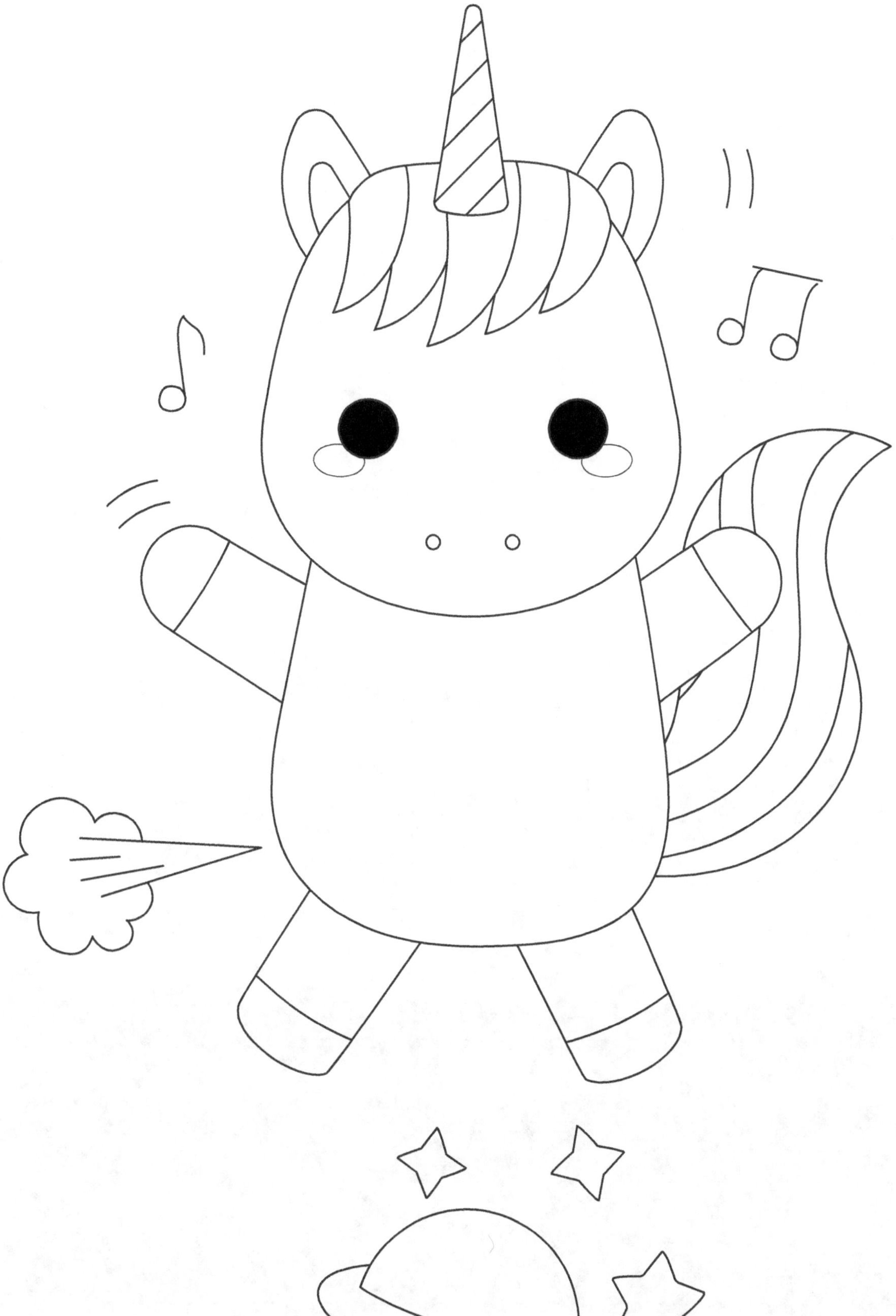

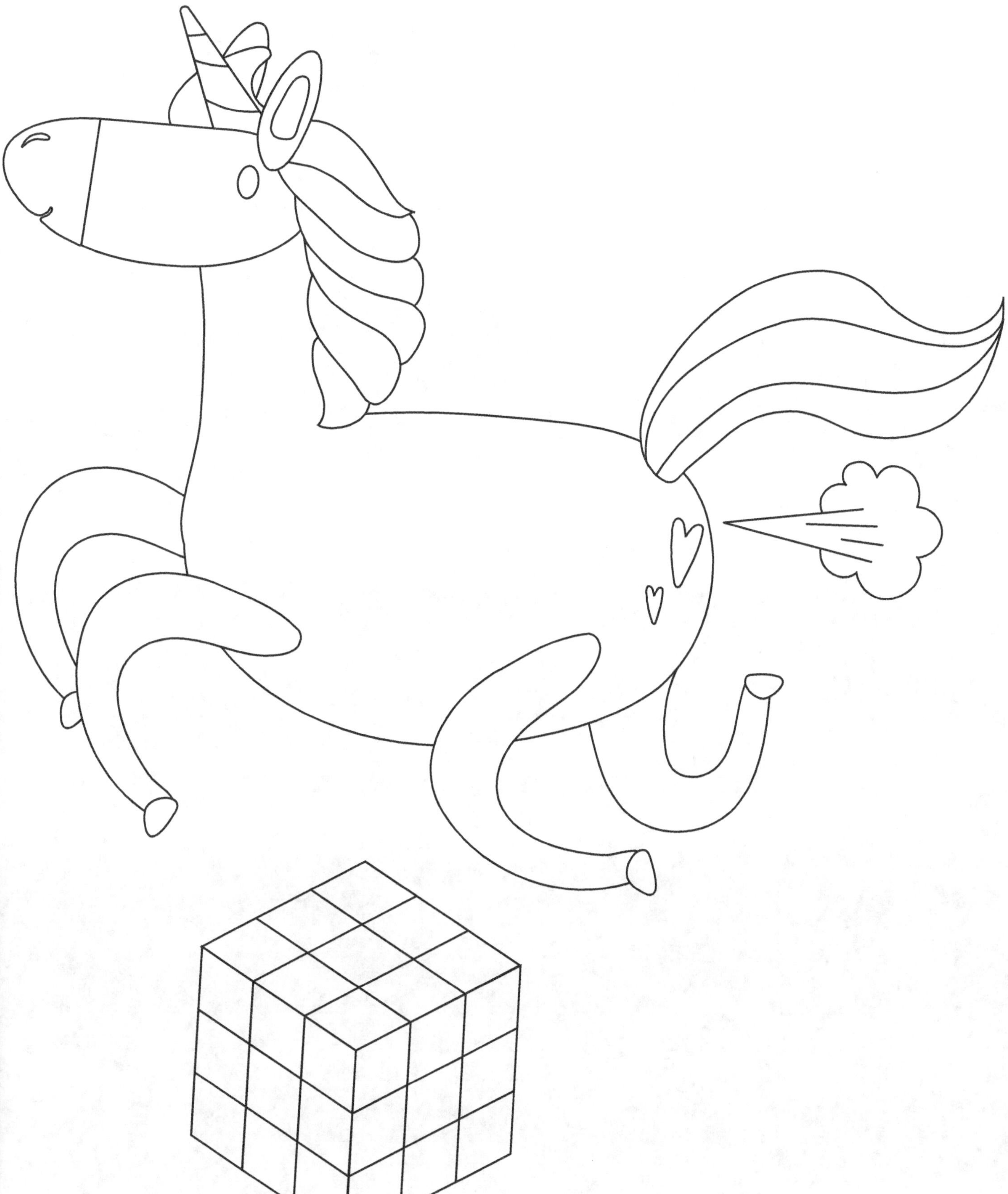

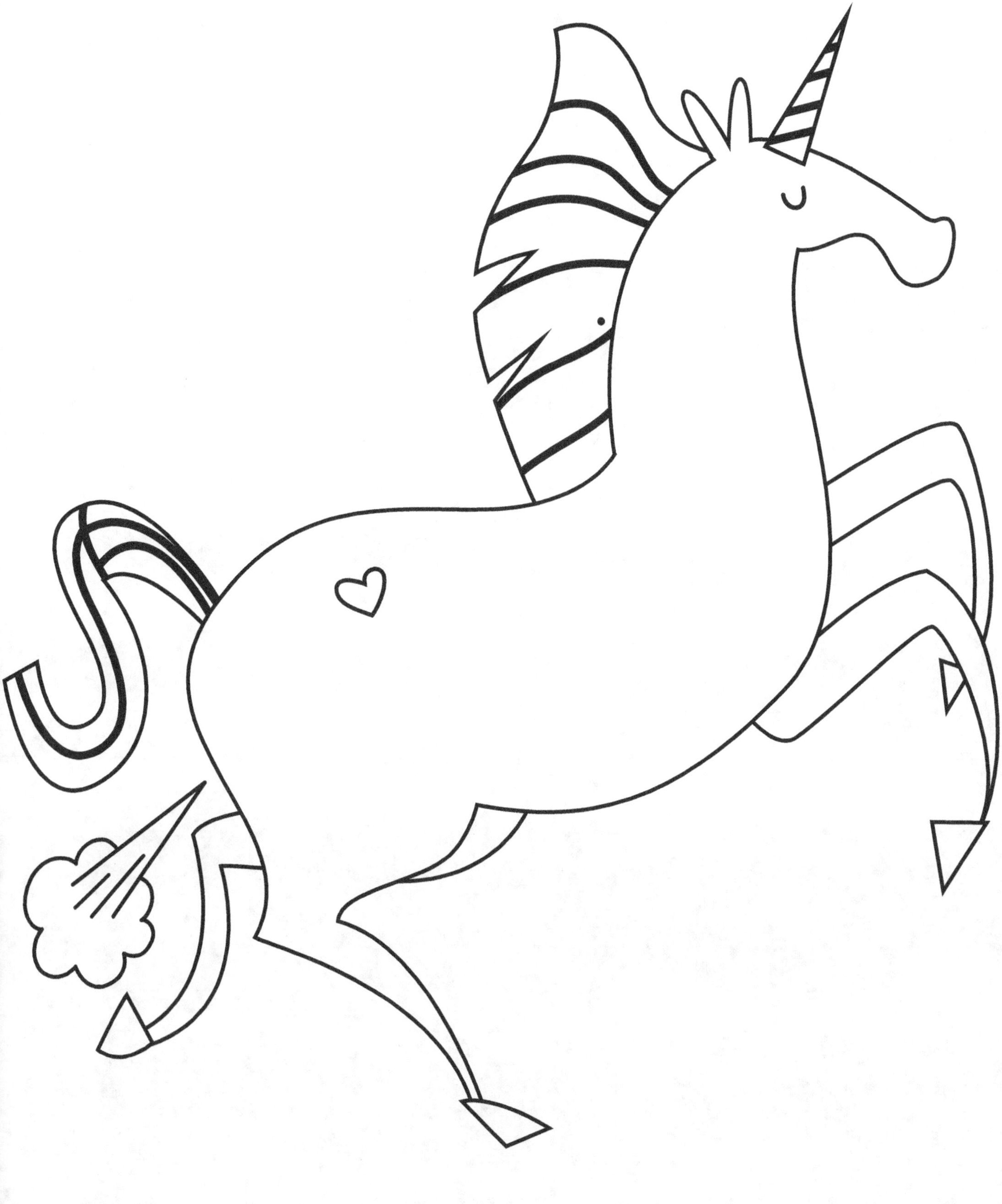

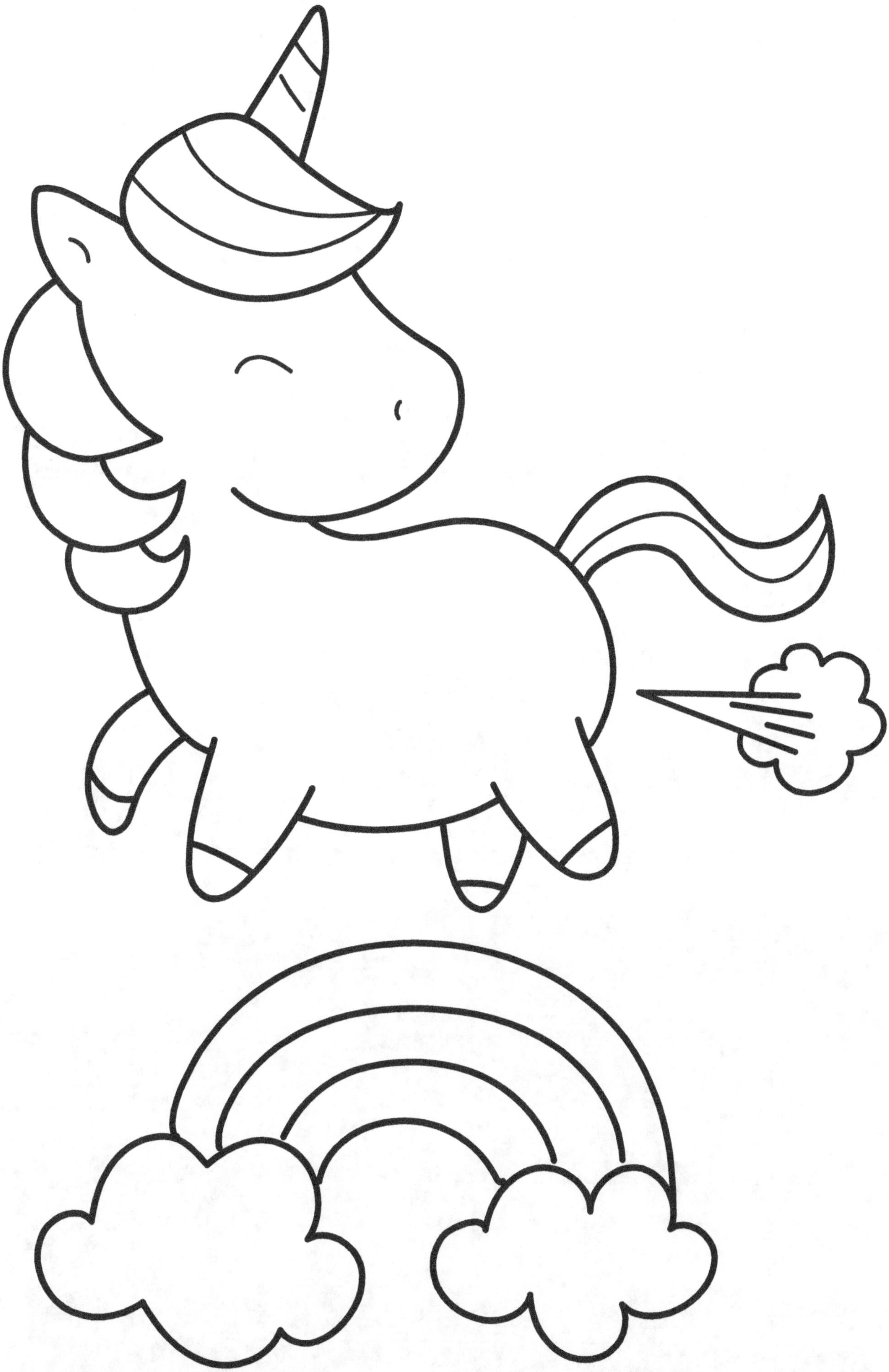

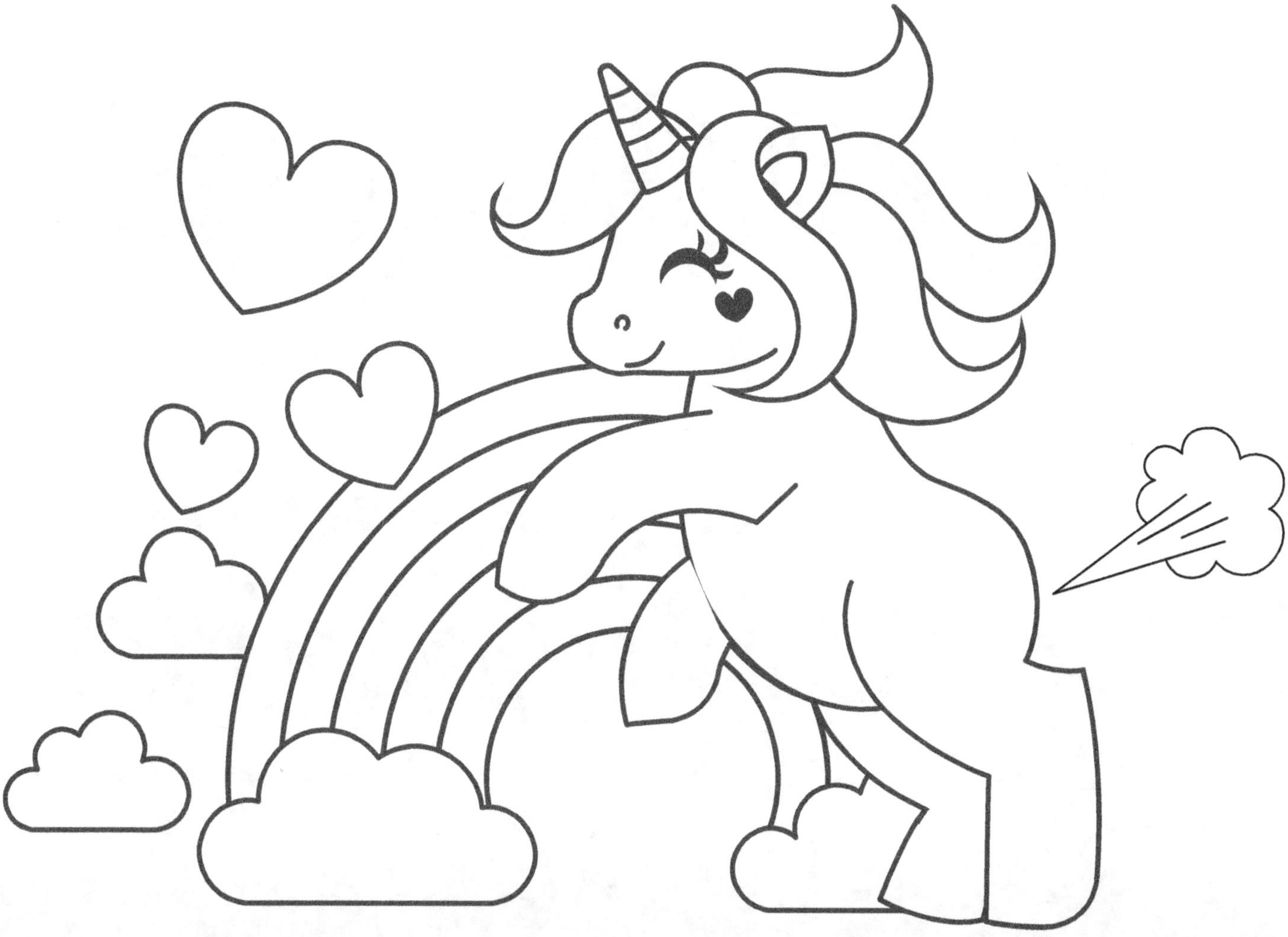

www.ingramcontent.com/pod-product-compliance
Lightning Source LLC
Chambersburg PA
CBHW081024170526
45158CB00010B/3146